Software Versus Capital

John Ohno

November 27, 2019

Contents

introduction

Chapter 1

Introduction

The book you have before you is in some ways a companion piece to my earlier essay collection, *Big and Small Computing*. It has some overlap in content, and some overlap in themes. Like that book, it is a collection of my previously-published essays. Unlike that book, here I do not give concrete technical descriptions of computing systems. Instead, this book is composed primarily of short essays and manifestoes on the subject of the economic and cultural dimensions of software.

The first half of this book focuses on the unique ability of software to free us from capitalism, while the second half contains essays about licensing, community management, and intellectual development. market-myths-good-bad-and-bazaar

Chapter 2

Market Myths: Good, Bad, and Bazaar

The stories that hold up western* capitalism

first-a-procedural-note

2.1 First, a procedural note...

The truth value of a myth doesn't matter, where efficacy is concerned. However, some myths have become so strongly internalized that they become difficult to identify as myths; they are mistaken for "common sense". For most of us, the ideas underlying western* capitalism are like this. It's difficult to separate ourselves from these myths and gain the appropriate distance, so I'm going to engage in a little bit of 'debunking'—specifically, I'm going to take some time pointing out parts of the capitalist model that don't match with reality or history, during the course of analyzing its structure and function. This doesn't take away from the immense power and importance of capitalist mythology, nor does it indicate that I consider all of the ideas associated with capitalism to be strictly false.

on-tautology

2.2 On tautology

Academics tend to treat tautologies as a lesser form. Tautologies are shallow, by their nature. It's quite reasonable for a system optimizing for novel and interesting ideas to reject tautologies. Nevertheless, some really important ideas can be rephrased as tautologies—as Charles Fort points out, natural selection is better summarized as "survival of the survivors" than "survival of the fittest"—and one can make the argument that any really true argument is in some sense circular. There's no shame in a circular argument that depends only on true premises. In fact, this is one way to look at all of mathematics—which is true because of its internal consistency, and only accidentally coincides with physical reality.

When someone dismisses a seemingly profound statement as "just a tau-

This essay was originally published in Modern Mythology. Thanks to James Curcio for editing the version found there

* "Western" is neither precise nor correct here. These myths seem to be present in western Europe, North America, Japan, and South Korea. Both China and the former Soviet states have different mythology I'm not qualified to analyse. In the absence of a better term than "western capitalism", I will use it.

5

tology" they omit important information. An obvious tautology contains no information. However, a non-obvious tautology is just about the most profound thing imaginable—it takes a complex, incomplete, vague collection of loosely related ideas and replaces it with a much smaller and simpler set of rules, which (if the tautology is reasonably close to correct) is both at least as accurate as the original set of ideas and easier to reason about. A non-obvious true tautology refactors huge sections of our mental models. Obviousness is a function of existing knowledge, so what is an obvious tautology to some people will be non-obvious to others. It should come as no surprise that people seek out ideas that present themselves as non-obvious tautologies.

The drive toward seeking non-obvious tautologies can lead to mistakes. Looking for simple and efficient models of the world is a mechanism for enabling lazy thinking. When lazy thinking is correct it's strictly superior to difficult thinking, but lazy thinking often comes with lazy meta-cognition. If we jump on ideas that look like non-obvious tautologies too greedily, we fail to see hidden assumptions.

Market efficiency is a very attractive model. Under certain circumstances, we can expect things to actually work that way. If a large number of competing producers really do start off completely even in capability, we really can expect the best product to price ratio to win out. To accept it completely means ignoring hidden assumptions that serious thinkers should at least consider.

One hidden assumption in market efficiency is that competitors start off even in capability. This is almost never the case outside of a classroom demonstration. Companies enter established markets and compete with established competitors, and companies established in one market will enter another. Both of these mechanisms make use of existing resource inequality in order to reduce precisely the kinds of risks that lead to efficient markets, and while perhaps in the long run poor products might lose out, with the extreme spread of resource availability the "long run" can easily last until long after we are all dead. Given no other information, if age is not normally or logarithmically distributed, we can reasonably expect something to last about twice as long as it already has. With corporations, the tails of this distribution are further apart—we can expect a startup to be on its last legs, and we can expect a 50 year old company to last 75 more years, because resource accumulation corrects for risks. A company that has a great deal of early success can coast on that success for a much longer period of poor customer satisfaction.

Another hidden assumption is that communication is free within the set of consumers and between consumers and producers but not within the set of producers.

Free communication within the set of producers is called collusion, and the SEC will hit you with an antitrust suit if you are found to engage in it. People do it all the time, and it is usually worth the risk, since it reduces market efficiency down to almost zero.

Free communication between producers and consumers is also pretty rare: even failing producers typically have too many consumers to manage individually and must work with lossy and biased aggregate information; successful producers have enough resources to be capable of ignoring consumer demand for quite a while, and often encourage 'customer loyalty' via branding. (In other words, cultivating a livestock of people who will buy their products regardless of quality—ideally enough to provide sufficient resources that appealing to the rest of the customers is unnecessary). Customer loyalty can have its benefits compounded if wealthy customers are targeted: "luxury brands" are lucrative because something can be sold well above market price regardless of its actual quality or desirability, and sometimes the poor price/desirability ratio is actually the point (as a form of lekking / conspicuous consumption).

Free communication between consumers is becoming more and more rare, since flooding consumer information channels with fake reviews and native advertising is cheap and easy. There used to be stronger social and economic incentives to clearly differentiate advertising from word of mouth, but advertising's effectiveness has dropped significantly as customers develop defenses against it and economic instability has encouraged lots of people to lower their standards. Eventually, consumer information channels will become just as untrusted as clearly paid advertising is now considered to be, and communication between consumers will be run along the same lines as cold war espionage.

motivated-reasoning

2.3 Motivated reasoning

Considering that the hidden assumptions in market efficiency are dependent upon situations even uninformed consumers know from experience are very rare, why would people accept it so easily? The inefficiency of markets has no plausible deniability, but motivated reasoning lowers the bar for plausibility significantly.

During the bulk of the 20th century we could probably argue that anticommunist propaganda played a large role. I don't think that's true anymore. Nevertheless, in many circles faith in the invisible hand actually is increasing.

There's another kind of circular reasoning—one that operates on the currency of guilt and hope. If one accepts market efficiency, it tells the poor that they can rise up through hard work, and it tells the rich that they earned their wealth. This is remarkably similar to the prosperity gospel, which claims that god rewards the righteous with wealth and therefore the poor must have secret sins. It also resembles the mandate of heaven, which claims that all political situations are divinely ordained and therefore disagreeing with the current ruler is sinful.

The similarity between the guilt/hope axis of the market efficiency myth and the prosperity gospel explains the strange marriage between Randian Objectivists and Evangelical Christians found in the religious right. We can reasonably expect many members of this group to be heavily motivated by the desire to believe that the world is fair. It's not appropriate to characterize this movement as lacking in empathy—empathy is a necessary prerequisite for a guilt so extreme that it makes an elaborate and far-fetched framework for victim-blaming look desirable.

For the poor of this movement, at least on the prosperity gospel side, it might not be so terrible. Motivating a group of people to do the right thing has a good chance of actually improving life generally, even if their promised reward never materialized; second order effects from accidental windfalls are more dangerous, though. (For instance, if you disown your gay son and then win the lottery, you're liable to get the wrong idea about what "doing the right thing" means).

That said, while the above factors encourage people to trust more strongly in an idea of market efficiency they already accept, bootstrapping the idea of market efficiency is much more difficult.

natural-law-myth-vs-legend

2.4   Natural law, myth vs legend

Market efficiency draws power from an older myth: the idea that money is a natural and universal means of exchange. This is historically and anthropologically dubious. David Graeber, in his book Debt: The First 5,000 Years, makes an argument for the idea that systematic accounting of debts predates the use of actual currency and furthermore only became necessary when cities became large enough to necessitate something resembling modern bureaucracy. Regardless of how accurate that timeline is, we know that gift economies, potlatch, and feasting are more common in tribal nomadic societies than any kind of currency exchange, and that feasting in particular remained extremely important in Europe through the Renaissance.

The legend that backs up the myth of money-as-natural-law takes place in a town. A shoemaker trades shoes for potatoes, but doesn't want potatoes, so he organizes a neutral currency so that potatoes and apples can be traded for shoes. Graeber points out that this level of specialization couldn't be 'natural'—the town is an appropriate place to set it, since specializing in a particular crop or craft would have been suicidal in the bands of 20–50 people that most humans lived in prior to around 2000 BC.

Our first examples of writing, of course, coincide with the first permanent settlements to have a large enough population to justify heavy specialization. Our first examples of writing are, in fact, spreadsheets recording debt and credit. This, along with the evidence that the unit of currency (the mina of silver) was too substantial for most people to afford even one of (and probably was mostly moved between rooms in the temple complex), is part of Graeber's argument that independent individuals carrying money for the purpose of direct transactions (i.e., our conception of money) probably only became common later, when imperial armies were expected to feed themselves in foreign lands.

So, on the one hand, it seems to have taken a very long time for the 'natural' 'common sense' concept of money to take hold among humans. On the other hand, people exposed to the idea of money tend to adapt to it quickly and we have even been able to teach apes to exchange tokens between themselves in exchange for goods and services—in other words, it's a simple and intuitive system that even animals we mostly don't consider conscious can grasp.

If something is considered natural law, it's very easy for people to believe that it is also providence. If something is straightforward and useful in every day life, it's very easy for people to consider it natural law.

moral-economies

2.5 Moral economies

Thoughtful economists tend to recognize the caveats I present here. Some behavioral economists have done great work on illuminating what kinds of things aren't—or shouldn't be—subject to the market. This, in turn, illuminates the market myth itself.

It's possible to think of social relations as economic in nature. Indeed, this is a pretty common model. Transactional psychology presents social interactions as the exchange of a currency of strokes, for instance. Nevertheless, Khaneman presents an experiment that shows social relations aren't, and shouldn't, be fungible.

The experiment went like this: a busy day care center has a problem with parents picking up their children late, and instates a fee. Parents in turn respond by picking up their kids late more often, and paying the fee. After the fee is eliminated, the percentage of on-time pickups does not return to the pre-fee state.

Khaneman interprets the results in this way: initially, parents thought of picking their kids up late as incurring a social debt (they were guilty about inconveniencing the day care), the fee reframed it as a service (they can pay some money in exchange for their kids being watched a little longer, guilt-free). But when the fee was eliminated, they felt as though they were getting the service for free.

This result looks a whole lot like the way fines for immoral business practices end up working.

If we consider that, typically, we can make up to people we feel we have wronged, we consider social currency to be somewhat fungible. Nevertheless, exchanging money for social currency is still mostly taboo—paying for sex is widely considered taboo, and even those of us who feel no taboo about sex work would find the idea of someone paying someone else to be their friend a little disturbing. If my best friend helps me move furniture and I give him a twenty dollar bill, he might be insulted. If I left money on the dresser after having sex with my girlfriend, she might be insulted. (Or consider it a joke.)

We could consider the ease with which money is quantified to be the problem. We rarely can put a number on our guilt or joy. On the other hand, we can generally determine if we feel like we've "done enough" to make up for something—our measures of social currency have ordinality, if not cardinality.

Instead, the disconnect is that money is, by design, impersonal. I cannot pay back my guilt over Peter by giving him Paul's gratitude toward me. This is where transactional psychology's monetary metaphor for strokes falls apart: a relationship is built up via the exchange of strokes, and that relationship has value based on trust. Meanwhile, any currency has, as a key feature, the ability to operate without trust or even with distrust. Money makes living under paranoia possible, and sometimes even pleasant. But exchange of strokes has its own inherent value, and the trust it builds likewise: it cannot be replaced with money because money's value is based only on what it can buy.

speculation

2.6 Speculation

The belief in market efficiency, and the emotional and moral dimensions of that belief, have some unfortunate consequences in speculation. Paradoxically, these consequences are opposed by the myth of money as natural law.

With speculation, one can create money without substance. Promises, bets, and hedges can be nested indefinitely to create value held in superposition. A stake in a speculative market is both credit and debt until it is sold. This is natural, since social constructs are eldrich, operating on fairy logic. This is both a pot of gold and a pile of leaves until I leave the land of the sidhe. Of course, there's every incentive to oversell, so more often than not it's a pile of leaves: when too many superpositions collapse, so does the market.

Naive materialism, when it intersects with the idea of money as natural law, finds the eldrich nature of money in speculation disturbing. Isn't money gold? Or coins? How can something be in my hand and then disappear? So, we get arguments for the gold standard along moral lines: "it's immoral for something that's real to behave like fairy dust, so we should limit its growth to match mining efficiency".

The eldrich behavior of money has some paradoxical results. Being aware that money is a social construct tends to decrease its value (clap your hands if you believe!). The question "if someone burns a million quid on TV, does the value of the pound go up or down" is very had to answer. (If you think you know the answer, substitute a million for a trillion, or for twenty.) On the other hand, being aware of its eldrich nature also tends to slightly decouple one from potentially-destructive drives.

Belief in market efficiency leads successful speculators to believe themselves skilled. While skill at speculation might be possible, statisticians who have studied the problem have generally come to the conclusion that the success distribution is adequately explained by market speculation being entirely random. Unwarranted confidence can lead to larger bets, which (if results are random) means half the time the money disappears into thin air. This does not require malfeasance, misrepresentation, or willful ignorance (as with the 2008 housing crisis). Believing that speculation involves skill is sufficient to cause the market to have larger and larger bubbles and crashes. software-vs-capital

Chapter 3

Software vs Capital

I have periodically said "software has nothing to do with business" as a criticism of tech journalism that focuses on firms and corporate politics over tech itself, or that considers all software to be products or potential products, or that considers success to be defined primarily in terms of money. I get a lot of pushback, including from intelligent tech journalists who I feel should understand my criticisms, so I'd like to expand on my quip.

When I say 'luckily software has nothing to do with business', I do not mean that business is irrelevant to software in practice. What I mean is that software is uniquely positioned, compared to all other engineering, to be free of economies of scale: it is cheap to develop and has near zero cost of reproduction. Business has the capacity to be irrelevant to software without any radical changes to how business is run or software is developed in practice.

In other words, software development can be done outside a capitalist context to a much greater extent than material forms of tinkering. Coding is not an expensive hobby: only the free-time component applies. Even a fairly weak form of UBI could give a big boost to free software, because most available software (still) is not developed by businesses or for business purposes but as a hobby by hobbyists who expect nothing in exchange.

I am not claiming that software engineering for the money is somehow illegitimate. I consider the entire 'work to live' arrangement to be illegitimate. Software engineering, like writing, benefits more from the abolition of that arrangement because of the combination of low resource costs & a lot of people willing to do it for fun.

The purchase of a physical computer for the sake of developing software is much like the purchase of a typewriter for the purpose of writing a novel: it is a large one-time cost, after which only small incidental costs are incurred (paper and ink, or power and internet), and it is a cost that most people have already paid. You can use the same computer for a decade or two. Other technical hobbies (like knitting or electronics) have much larger ongoing material costs— and even near-ubiquitous situations like car ownership are much more onerous in this respect.

Amusingly, the very attributes that make it possible for something to escape from capitalist domination also make it particularly desirable to Capital. The elevation of sign or Spectacle over reality is like Capital engaging its death drive, since value is wholly imaginary.

The logic of markets depends upon the (strictly incorrect but historically mostly good-enough) notion that there's some natural value to things, inherent to them and stable, which can be determined by looking at what people are willing to pay. When use value is the primary factor, sure. When labor value is the primary factor, sure. When the primary factor is speculative (what other people are predicted to be willing to pay), cost becomes totally unstable. This instability is mostly unpredictable. Of course, anybody who bets on instability and wins is going to attribute that to skill or insight, and since losing money is harder than making it once you're rich, they can remain unchallenged in this attribution. But, there is no major insight factor—merely survivorship bias. The winners win bigger and the losers lose more as we become untethered from the world and get stuck in never-never land, where the tinkerbell effect is the only law.

In other words, speculation is the end of those elements of markets that have ever been generally beneficial, but since they are overconfidence-generating machines, Capital is pulled into their gravity. I think we're past the event horizon here already. IP is a lot like speculation: the value of social constructions is usually dominated by social constructions, as production & marginal costs approach zero.

"Software is eating the world" is maybe better phrased as "The Spectacle is eating the End of History".

Why hasn't the essential spookiness of software eaten capital yet? I think a big part of this is an accident of history: the ascent of the web as the highest-profile hypertext system at the same time the ban on commercial use of the internet was lifted. The use of host-oriented addressing in URLs, while non-problematic in smaller networks where the number of viewers has a low upper limit, produces problems when the number of viewers becomes large. Making even a static website scale to extremely large numbers of requests requires expensive hardware, because all the requests must be tricked into thinking they are connecting to a single machine with a single address, even in situations where a single machine of arbitrary power couldn't possibly serve all of them. This opens up a convenient opportunity for rent-seeking: anyone with sufficient capital can provide the expensive hardware necessary for working around the web's broken scaling, and so we get hosting services, data center services like AWS, and cache services like CloudFlare.

Even free/open source software, nominally isolated from the constraints of capital, typically makes use of host-oriented URL schemes and the host-oriented assumptions that come with them. Projects get hosted by github, or pay for domain names and get hosted in data centers. In this way, these projects shore up the finances of the merchants of scale, slumlords of the internet.

I expect that if named-data networking systems like IPFS, sneakernet-capable social network systems like Secure Scuttlebutt, & alternatives to for-profit ISPs like mesh networks & long-range wifi become popular among the numerati, we'll see an acceleration of Capital's slow sinking into masturbatory irrelevance in the domain of software & computer technologies. Even if you don't have personal reasons to support these kinds of technologies (such as a concern for privacy and autonomy), I recommend supporting them on the grounds of seizing the means of computation.

You have nothing to lose but your blockchains. conditions-for-the-possibility-of-exit

Chapter 4

Conditions for the possibility of exit

a-response-to-the-conversations-that-cryptocurrency-killed-by-sonya-mann

4.1 A response to *The Conversations that Cryptocurrency Killed* by Sonya MannA response to The Conversations that Cryptocurrency Killed by Sonya Mann

Exit (and the right to exit) is fundamentally important and too-often ignored. But, we should be careful to be clear about to what extent we exit, and how. Many technologies that are promoted as revolutionary tools don't actually provide the capacity for exit in the way they seem to at first glance. Had the article been called 'The Conversations that Encryption Killed', I would not feel the need to respond, but the 'crypto' prefix in 'cryptocurrency' is misleading and bitcoin-style distributed-public-ledger-based systems are not compatible with anything more than a 'limited, voice-buttressed exit'.

When we perform a true exit, we have made ourselves no longer subject to the power structure we have exited from. In the politico-social domain, there are several power structures we might want to exit: the domination of the state (i.e., the rule of law), the domination of finance (i.e., dependence upon existing systems of trade for the means of survival), and the domination of old money (i.e., existing debts, and the advantages produced by access to money in the past). Cryptocurrencies do not provide the conditions for the possibility of exit from any of these three power structures, in part because of myopia in both the technical and cultural design of bitcoin and in part because of the fungibility of power.

Cryptocurrencies based on public ledgers do not provide an exit from the rule of law, nor do they provide an effective cover for trade; they are, in fact, more easily traceable than cash. This is because they are not in fact anonymous but pseudonymous—every wallet has a permanent address, and every entity has at least one wallet—and because all pseudonymous transfers are recorded

Sonya's essay can be found at `https://jacobitemag.com/2018/07/27/the-conversations-that-cryptocurrency-kills/`

permanently and publicly in the ledger. This sacrifices secrecy in favor of limiting necessary trust.

There is no cryptography-like guarantee on the difficulty of tracing a transaction history: doing so simply takes linear time with respect to the number of global transactions within the period you're looking for. Laundering of money through third party mixers is rare, because the culture of bitcoin has paranoia as a design philosophy—while laundering could make tracing transactions meaningfully harder, it only does so if it becomes common, and it will only become common if there is some guarantee that mixers won't run away with your money (precisely the kind of guarantee that can't be made within the system itself without sacrificing the secrecy it provides). Escrow has become fairly common, but it has exactly the same problem as mixers without providing the functional secrecy (or the ability to be chained) that mixers provide.

Ultimately, using a public-ledger-based cryptocurrency means 'opening the books' to literally everyone and making a permanent public record of all your purchases—something that, with only a relatively small amount of information, can be traced to your legal identity. In other words, the only exit from state domination made possible by this kind of cryptocurrency is 'limited and voice-buttressed': with careful opsec (a full time job, & one that professionals regularly fail at) you might be able to make it difficult to trace your wallet back to your public persona, but your only real defense is to make yourself an unappealing target by staying within the law most of the time.

This is not, in fact, something shared with all alternative currencies. Physical alternative currencies are often very difficult to trace, and when commodities are used as currencies (like bottles of Tide, baby formula, or lego sets) there's also plenty of plausible deniability. If you actually want your transactions to remain secret, perform them in laundry detergent, not bitcoin.

It's hardly surprising that cryptocurrencies will not save us from the domination of finance—they are, after all, currencies. Most boosters of cryptocurrencies don't see this as a bug. But, to be clear: the use of cryptocurrencies does not even allow us the possibility of escape into an alternate market-universe where goods and services have fair prices without exploitation; even if this was the goal of some set of cryptocurrency users and they were all agreed on it, the fact that this currency can be traded for another kind or for goods produced within the regular (exploitative) capitalist system means that such an exit is limited and voice-buttressed at best: the only way to ensure your economy remains fair is to exile anyone who tries to connect it to the wider world. (This is again not actually true of all trade. The pseudo-economy of reputation is resistant to fungibility within peer groups—someone who tries to use their resources to create a false sense of integrity or trustworthiness is quickly found out and shunned, and this happens without any kind of central planning or formal rules.)

This brings us to the domination of old money. Fungibility is the enemy here, too: whatever debt you might have had before you started doing all your transactions in bitcoin still exists, and whatever wealth you might have had can be traded for bitcoin. You can be asked to repay your debts in bitcoin.

Since the publication of this essay, I have been informed that some cryptocurrencies (including ZCash, which Sonya represents at the time of this writing) have solved the problem of public ledgers being tracable, though not the other problems dealt with in this essay. These technical solutions to traceability rely on complex cryptography which may turn out to be more fragile than expected. In fact, in the year since I initially wrote this essay, ZCash has been discovered to have a vulnerability (CVE-2019-16930) that leaked this information, as well as another vulnerability that allowed counterfieting. These have been patched, but the sheer complexity of cryptoanalysis makes it difficult for individuals without an extremely strong background to trust the security of novel cryptosystems: after all, experts did not catch these through multiple audits.

Whether or not you were able to afford to go to college determines whether or not you can make bitcoin as much as it did with regard to whether or not you can make dollars.

Furthermore, cryptocurrencies do not even stem further exaggeration of inequity in initial conditions: just as with dollars, those who have plenty of bitcoin have access to more effective ways of increasing their wealth—methods that no amount of merit or hard work can compete with.

Perhaps even more problematic: cryptocurrencies fail, in the same way as fiat currency, to counter the attractive force between wealth and power, whereby the powerful achieve wealth without sacrificing their power and the wealthy achieve power without sacrificing their wealth. The gravitational pull of wealth-power brings in expensive gifts (which can be re-sold or re-gifted or simply used to attract social status), favors (a kind of power which does not need to be paid for and can be turned into money if re-gifted or used for material gain), subservience (a kind of power given out of fear), and the ear of a wider community of the wealthy and powerful.

This is not true of all alternative market systems: potlatches transform wealth into power or social standing while wiping the wealth out (since the lavish gifts given during a potlatch are literally destroyed), while jubilees remove debts without wiping out credits; negative interest lessens the advantages of the already-wealthy, while a negative income tax lessens the disadvantages of the poor.

Cryptocurrency does not represent a functional exit from modern global power structures any moreso than Burning Man does: it merely represents a pantomime of exit, with the aesthetics of radical politics but none of the substance.

freeing-software

For more information on these vulnerabilities, see: * http://duke.leto.net/2019/10/01/zcash-metadata-leakage-cve-2019-16930.html * https://electriccoin.co/blog/zcash-counterfeiting-vulnerability-successfully-remediated/

Chapter 5

Freeing software

The noble goal of the free software movement is to change the relationship between people & software and to change the relationships between people mediated by software—specifically, to make software work for people by removing legal barriers based on intellectual property law that arbitrarily separate user from developer, so that users can change software to suit their own needs.

(In practice, free software has attained this utopian ideal in only a limited scope. This is not the appropriate place to dig deeply, but suffice it to say that because of myopia & a misplaced pragmatism, in the form of an unwillingness to address barriers other than IP, free software caters almost exclusively to professional developers looking for a free drop-in replacement for a commercial product to use in the course of their lucrative work creating other commercial products. Utopia for the few is a kind of dystopia.)

The legal barriers between user and developer have historically been erected almost exclusively in the name of commerce. While the depoliticized & commerce-friendly 'open source' movement has only worked to demolish the barriers separating large companies from unpaid labor, the free software movement has continued to patch new exploits deployed by the forces of capital to subvert ostensibly free software into a position of user hostility in the form of various means to avoid sharing code improvements: GPL3 patched away various loopholes in linking to proprietary code, and Afferro GPL patched away the ability to avoid 'distribution' entirely by deploying as a service.

These patches do not and can not address the root of the problem: users and corporations do not have aligned incentives, and capital produces an exponential distribution of power asymmetry (the only thing in computing that really doubles every 18 months is the accumulated ability to coerce the skilled labor of engineers); therefore, so long as capital has the ability & incentive to influence software production, software will be pitted against users.

Here's a simple example. I am a user of Linux—which is free software. This means that, theoretically, I can spend an hour or two after work modifying Linux to better suit my own needs—assuming I have the energy. I am lucky, as a professional developer; I don't work nearly as hard as a cashier or a burger flipper, and unlike those people, I get a living wage and paid vacation. So, I have much more time to adapt Linux to my needs, including learning whatever I need to learn to do that. But IBM can afford to employ hundreds of people full time to modify Linux in order to make it better fit for IBM's needs. In fact, IBM, Google, Apple, Microsoft, and NVIDIA all pay people to work full time on Linux & all the various associated pieces of code, and while their work very occasionally benefits me, it mostly benefits other big companies & often makes things worse for me. After all, my ability to use my desktop doesn't benefit at all from scaling optimizations (it's not part of a cluster, I'm not doing high performance computing on it, and it matters a lot more to me in practice that a web page is unresponsive than that it's taking ten seconds less to compile GCC), & the way a Linux box is deployed and manipulated at scale (containerization, remote manipulation of firmware) ranges from irritant to potential vulnerability when applied to a self-administered personal machine.

Every open source project that is marginally amenable to the needs of capital gets further biased toward corporate use, unless (as in the case of openssl & other packages that really require serious professional expertise) they are already so optimized for use by a rareified class of professional software developers that even large corporations find it easier to simply use them than to contribute to them (at which point they will simply be adopted when the maintainer inevitably starves to death or runs out of dialysis money).

As someone who values the goals of free software, what can I do? The FSF won't save me: they have been in bed with capital since Cygnus; the OSI was in bed with capital from the beginning.

My preferred solution is to write software so philosophically and structurally misaligned with the needs of capital that to be adopted by a commercial enterprise would require a substantial (preferably even total) rewrite. So much free & open source software is structured for easy consumption by corporations, sometimes because the packages are in fact money-making enterprises (through support contracts, dual licensing based freemium plans, or as a kind of loss-leader or PR boost), but often it's simply because when the author goes home and starts writing software he uses the unexamined habits picked up from the previous eight hours of writing software for The Man. Quirky, personal software that is aggressively unscalable & focuses on delivering human needs in human time over machine needs in machine time is nicer to write, nicer to use, and difficult for capital to subvert.

Anti-authoritarian anti-capitalist software structure requires care and introspection, though, & good-faith efforts like Mastodon still often fail. So, in a pinch, a 'no commercial use' clause will do—so long as it's combined with guaranteed basic income.

The only way to set software free is to unshackle it from the needs of capital. And, capital has become so dependent upon software that an independent ecosystem of anti-capitalist software, sufficiently popular, can starve it of access to the speed and violence it needs to consume ever-doubling quantities of to survive. free-software-and-the-revolt-against-transactionality

Chapter 6

Free software and the revolt against transactionality

In 1994, the electronic pop band KLF burned a million pounds—money they had earned by following instructions laid out in a book they wrote called "The Manual". To this day, they deny having a conscious justification for that powerful act. One possible interpretation is to see The Manual & the Burning as two sides of a single central thesis: a rejection of the connection between labor-value and price-value implied by money, through a violation of expectations of transactionality.

The Manual is a get-rich-quick scheme—one that worked brilliantly for the KLF. Burning a million pounds, on the other hand, was harrowing and difficult, and yet not only decreased their personal wealth but decreased the total amount of money in circulation. Money is expected to be exchanged, and while we accept slack (the term, from The Church of the SubGenius, for 'getting something for nothing'), we do not accept anti-slack (getting nothing for something). Getting rich quick implies getting poor quick in a system with a relatively-static or slowly-growing store of value, but we accept the idea that we can consitently earn profits while considering the kind of sudden disappearance of price-value that comes with market corrections (bubbles popping) as an anomaly—and so, intentionally destroying price-value comes off as a very radical act.

However, in a gift economy, the destruction of value of any kind is not only not radical but actually fundamental to the creation of norms. Free software was once this kind of gift economy.

Transactionality—the expectation that, under normal circumstances, to recieve an item one must exchange something of equal value—relies upon legibility. Things whose value cannot be verified cannot be exchanged except at a loss—based on the smallest guaranteed value. Popular mechanisms for counteracting the unpleasant side effects of capitalist transactionality—charity, welfare—tend to themselves be transactional: we try to determine who is most in need of our donation (and thus, who would maximize our sense of satisfaction in our own generosity), or we weigh candidates based on preferences (as though they were themselves products). Our society lacks the concepts of jubilee and potlatch (even though the central premise of several major religions is built on jubilee & potlatch).

Jubilee is a kind of anti-slack social release valve: periodically, at unpredictable intervals, creditors forgive all debts, and thus debtors are free from those obligations. (In the United States & elsewhere, some kinds of debts expire if you do not attempt to pay them for long enough, which acts as a kind of jubilee. Knowledge of this kind of debt expiration is not widespread; like jury nullification, it's a situation that empowers individuals while annoying enforcement.) Potlatch involves the exchange & destruction of elaborate gifts—a sacrifice in the name of cooperation, and a demonstration of the material ability to support a community—an ability limited to the resource-rich, who are expected to deliver on this implied promise.

Writing free software is a politically radical act: while software has low reproduction cost, both the use value and the initial labor value of good software is high, so putting it into the public domain is a kind of perpetual jubilee (those who use it do not owe the author anything in exchange for its use-value) and a potlatch in the sense that the labor is exchanged for nothing at all. Copyleft licenses are even more radical: all derived software remains free from the normal mechanisms that drive labor into a state of transactionality. Although one can sell free software, the cost of reproduction is so low (and the legal mechanisms for preventing reproduction so hamstrung by the license itself) that it makes more sense to treat paying for free software as a gift-in-kind, rather than an exchange.

The idea of "open source" changed this.

Since 2001, whole industries have grown out of the gifts of programmers, and these industries are dependent upon free software, without which they would not be profitable. Many of the programmers thought they were giving gifts to mankind, not to Google. Others had no such illusions: they were competing for positions in an industry where performing free labor of professional quality was an implied prerequisite for being hired. The current state of open source—inevitable from the beginning—is the exploitation of the expectation of free labor for the sake of propping up unprofitable businesses.

What kind of revolt could possibly shake these norms without getting rid of the (now endangered) gift economy of free software?

Software intended for businesses has a need that software intended for individuals does not: scalability. Software intended for individuals can be unstandardized, ad-hoc, quirky, and personal. 'Enterprise' software must pretend to scale (even if it cannot), & the centralization necessary for any business to make a profit increases the load on the software that inhabits that bottleneck.

For twenty years, we've been making corporations rich by buying into standardization and scale—making it feasible for them to funnel us into silos. We can stop this process, and perhaps even reverse it, by refusing to make unfrivolous software. Personal software should be personal: it should not scale or conform; it should chafe at strictures the same way you do, and burst out of any box that dare enclose it. a-qualified-defense-of-slacktivism

Chapter 7

A qualified defense of slacktivism

Slacktivism is a failure if you consider it to be a form of activism, but as a form of value signalling, it is terribly effective. We underestimate the value of signalling at our peril.

Some parts of our moral landscape appear to be biological in origin: a revulsion reaction to the idea of incest, for instance, appears to be the result of the sexual imprint process (and we can tell because siblings separated at birth actually have a much higher likelihood of ending up together, while unrelated children who spend a lot of time living together prior to puberty, even in non-family settings like boarding schools, have unnaturally low rates of sleeping together as adults). Others, however, seem to be primarily controlled by culture, specifically by cultural manipulation of empathy and shame. (We dehumanize enemies in war via propaganda, in order to eliminate the empathy we might normally have toward them & the shame we might hold for killing them, and instead substitute a new set of rules around what kinds of killings are shameful. If the domain over which empathy operated was biologically determined, the flexibility that makes modern warfare possible would not exist.)

Some people lack empathy (or its effect on them is abnormally low), just as some people lack the in-built biological drive to avoid incest. Shame works to police such people. Ultimately, shame serves to punish people who engage in violations of a culture's idea of moral behavior by lowering social status (and with it, access to various resources—particularly, other people). While we should still be concerned about sociopaths (who have a strange sort of superpower: their actions are not constrained by the force of empathy, and they lack the self-control to respond reliably to shame), the worst excesses of garden variety empathy-deficient narcissists can be avoided by judicious application of social pressures.

Value and virtue signalling is a major way in which a culture indicates what behaviors are considered acceptable and what behaviors are not considered acceptable. The other major way in which acceptable behaviors are signalled is punishment; however, punishment requires that the behavior be practiced and the culprit be caught. Value signalling might include describing counterfactuals or hypotheticals about punishment for breach of acceptable behavior (ranging from fantastical visions of hell to fairly concrete legal sentencing guides).

Slacktivism is a form of weak value signalling, wherein large numbers of people expend small amounts of effort in a token representation of the ideal behavior. While strong / costly signalling would send a more powerful message, it's not accessible to most people, and so the number of people engaging in it will necessarily always be small. Weak value signalling, at scale, is actually more potent: after all, costly signalling is more desirable both to those with sufficient resources that the marginal cost of signalling is smaller than its apparent cost to its target audience (philanthropists) and those with nothing to lose for whom costly signalling also represents an out (terrorists), neither of whom can be trusted to be an accurate representation of group norms. Mass action, on the other hand, is group norms embodied, and low social cost makes scale possible. As a result, slacktivism allows small changes in moral values to propogate quickly from the majority who already accept them to the minority who haven't yet, in much the same way as the Game of Life: if you're surrounded locally by people who send a particular signal, you're more likely to send that signal, until the signal reaches some saturation point.

Slacktivism, by changing the collective value system, also encourages acts of costly signalling in the same direction as that weak signal. Popular causes get donations (although the ratio of weak signals to strong signals will always be large).

Criticisms of slacktivism tend to hinge on the idea that it's a substitute for activism—that everyone who changes their profile picture to a flag might otherwise be staging a sit-in or assassinating a congressman or otherwise helping make real changes. But, slacktivism is better modeled as a form of collective social control of activism: a means by which various causes have their perceived importance ranked. a-qualified-defense-of-jargon-other-in-group-signifiers

Chapter 8

A Qualified Defense of Jargon & Other In-Group Signifiers

This essay is in part a response to an article I read this morning*. I won't link to the article, in part because I don't want to diminish it by talking over it, and in part because the story that this article tells is pretty common—plenty of people have complained about exactly the same thing, myself included. The article in question told the story of a self-taught programmer whose unfamiliarity with certain terms and historical figures theoretically irrelevant to her work marked her as an outsider & made her uncomfortable in a professional environment. I sympathize—after all, I too was once a self-taught developer in over my head, and I've gone through the process of trying to work in an environment where my unfamiliarity with the shibboleths marked me as an outsider. I also don't want to imply that her situation is justified—accidents of biology & history like gender, ethnicity, and childhood cultural background can make the bar for fitting into particular groups much higher than it should be. What I'd like to avoid is the shallow idea that we can just reject shibboleths altogether and solve all problems.

*September 2016

Jargon is a clear cut example of when a tool that's instrumental for competency also acts as a shibboleth. Most fields with complicated forms of technical knowledge also have specialized vocabulary or specialized meanings for particular words; the general consensus surrounding the meaning of a particular word stands in for a vast chunk of shared knowledge that would be complicated to explain in non-specialized language. When someone says "O(n)", they are making a claim that, in order to be understood, implies a familiarity with the calculus of derivatives, instruction counting, how loops work, and the idea of worst case versus expected case outcomes. Working with someone whose familiarity with foundational concepts in your field is at the level of an outsider is nearly impossible: you need to act the part of professor more often than you do real work; if someone lacks familiarity with the terminology, your handle for figuring out their knowledge level is no longer usable. Autodidacts are already at a disadvantage here: the set of things they know is not the same as that taught by a degree program, and they can have large conspicuous gaps in their knowledge even when it comes to relevant material. When an autodidact is unfamiliar with a term, it's hard to tell whether or not that indicates a gap in their competence that needs to be filled, taking up time and effort that could otherwise be applied to the ostensible end goal.

Even when a piece of jargon isn't of direct relevance, familiarity with jargon is indicative of a shared cultural experience that reflects shared values and habits—some pieces of which can be highly relevant. Using a term like "dot file" when referencing a hidden configuration file indicates familiarity and comfort with the unix environment, which might extend to a familiarity with pipes, standard unix tools, shell scripting, basic unix system administration, the history of the free software and open source movements, unix-style development toolchains, a preference for classic text editors like vi & emacs over graphical IDEs, an understanding of the unix philosophy of small modular programs working together on text streams, a familiarity with and preference for irc over other similar communication systems, a fondness for beards, and the ownership of toys shaped like penguins or tennis shoe wearing demons. Someone who just says "config file" will not open the floodgates of spurious cultural associations. (Likewise with "home directory" versus "user directory" or "my documents".) All of these associations are fuzzy: not everyone has equal immersion in the cultural ephemera related to some technology. However, there's a set of expectations associated with use of terminology: kinship with a set of tribes with clear centers and fuzzy boundaries.

Similarly, familiarity with certain historical figures has cultural relevance that extends to philosophy with meaningful applications in work environments. Somebody familiar with Djikstra who only learned about him in school probably only knows about him in the context of graph traversal, but someone familiar with Djikstra's mythology is likely to be familiar with a couple quotes: "asking if a computer can think is like asking if a submarine can swim" and "premature optimization is the root of all evil". Even if misattributed & misunderstood, both those quotes have impacts on the way someone develops software that go far beyond familiarity with graph traversal algorithms. Someone who quotes Postel's Law, similarly, has a particular philosophy that's easy to identify. All of these philosophies have impact, though the value of this impact depends on the application: Postel's Law was instrumental in both the widespread adoption of the world wide web and the horrible security shitshow that the world wide web can't extract itself from.

This is all to say that culture matters and signifiers matter. If you're working alone, it's fine to focus only on the precise technical ideas that stand between you and your immediate goal; as soon as you start working with a group, an inability to code switch means your coworkers can't predict your behavior, communicate with you efficiently about important things, or figure out what you need to know in order to do your job effectively. Hiring an autodidact is a big risk, which is why lots of places don't bother—it's not that a degree implies a high level of competence, but instead that a degree is a hedge against a low level of competence that would cost the company a lot of money; hiring an autodidact with big gaps in their understanding of jargon and culture is not merely a risk but an almost-guaranteed cost, even if the person in question has significantly above-average technical skills and work ethic.

All of this is a huge problem, because the tech industry has a number of problems related to a lack of diversity—particularly cultural diversity. We need to shake this industry up with outside ideas, and part of that is bringing in autodidacts who have experiences unlike those systematically manufactured by degree programs or accelerators. We need people who can point at the inconsistencies and stupidities that are passively accepted as normal by the monoculture. But, we need those people to speak the language.

If we don't throw away shibboleths entirely, what are we to do?

My recommendation is: outsiders, know your enemy. If you're learning to code on your own, pay attention to the mythology. Read the Jargon File. Read The Devouring Fungus. Read Hackers & Where Wizards Stay Up Late. Make sure that you have enough understanding of the history and culture to pass as a precocious newbie.

As for insiders: be conscious of the way shibboleths are being used. Just because someone doesn't know the term you used doesn't mean they are totally unfamiliar with the concept. Make sure you aren't leaning too heavily on spurious associations: playing Tempest doesn't really have anything to do with understanding depth-first searches, Stallman's association with Linux isn't much more than a series of accidents that don't meaningfully impact the syntax of awk, and LISP's vast mythology is mostly the product of it being really popular at MIT fifty years ago rather than some deep truth about lambda calculus. Make sure that, to the extent that you are using shibboleths as a proxy for competence, you are not doing so in a way that unfairly prevents competent outsiders from contributing meaningful work. And, especially, give the benefit of the doubt to anyone who isn't a cultural fit for reasons beyond their control: assume that women & people who are neither white nor asian are competent, because everyone else in their lives will assume they are incompetent.
in-defense-of-contempt

Chapter 9

In defense of contempt

A response to a popular article

The article in question suggests that the habitual tribalism & combative style in communication within the tech community is toxic, particularly to minorities; I do not dispute this point. The article in question also suggests that criticism of languages and technologies should be avoided because it often discourages community diversity, and this is where the author and I part ways.

The state of the programming community is poor, with regard to diversity, and this leads to all sorts of systematic problems that are self-perpetuating. However, the state of the programming ecosystem is also poor, and the perception of acceptability given to bad tooling and bad habits leads to systematic and self-perpetuating problems of its own. The way to increase acceptance of outsiders into the community is not by sacrificing the very worth of the enterprise the community exists to engage in; indeed, it's entirely unnecessary to do so.

The author decries the tribalism of the community with regard to tooling, but differences of opinion when it comes to preferred tools is not a meaningless aesthetic distinction. The prevalence of overflow-related vulnerabilities in real software ultimately comes down to the popularity of C over Pascal historically; as many exfiltrations of password files and other sensitive data are owed to the use of outdated PHP best practices as can be attributed to SQL injection (and thus, lack of input validation); the poor state of Windows security prior to 2001 when compared to competitors at the time ultimately comes down to the decision to avoid taking full and proper advantage of hardware memory management, setting up a proper system of user privileges, and other common practices in the domain of network-connected multi-user OSes—in other words, Windows was a leaky sieve and prime target for over a decade because lazy habits that were acceptable for single-user isolated machines with no real multitasking were being applied to a huge number of interconnected boxes.

The results of using a poor tool or using a good tool poorly are a lot like the results of ignoring modern medical science: in isolation, they might be acceptable for a handful of people who don't have it rough, but in aggregate

The article is not linked, to protect the innocent. We have all read articles like this one.

31

they result in epidemics. Someone who writes ostensibly production-ready code in PHP or Perl should be treated like someone who refuses to vaccinate their children: their behavior should be considered acceptable only if they are extremely careful and they have a very good excuse. Someone who promotes the use of tools that encourage the production of bug-prone insecure code outside the context of isolated personal experiments should be treated the same way we treat antivaxxers: as a perhaps well-meaning but deluded person whose misinformation is resulting in major destruction.

When someone has different aesthetic preferences, it's natural to accept that. But, when a group that is already marginalized disproportionately adopts a set of tools that are well-known to be destructive and then dedicates enormous resources to the use of those tools, we don't decide that those tools must be acceptable on aesthetic grounds despite their known destructive potential: we instead try to discourage that group from associating with those tools and figure out what forces are creating that association.

Poor tools are often the domain of beginners, and those who dedicate sufficient time and effort eventually graduate from those poor tools to better tools. (I first learned to program in QBasic.) That time and effort isn't free, so people who are already under other extra constraints (including people who have extra social or financial pressure) often never move on.

There's another factor here, however: good tools in some ways often become poor because they become popular with beginners. Most tools are optimized for a small set of problem domains, work acceptably in some others, and work horribly in every other domain. A beginner, having experience with only one tool, will apply this tool to every domain; if problems in some domain are harder to solve with this tool, the beginner, unless properly instructed, will believe the problems in this domain are simply inherently harder to solve. As a tool becomes popular with beginners, experts become difficult to identify in the crowd, and slightly elevated beginners begin to become treated like experts simply because there are many more slightly elevated beginners than experts; these pseudo-experts will popularize poor habits in the community, and these habits beocme associated with the tool itself. An expert who uses many tools will have less say in the community surrounding one tool than the many enthusiastic beginners who are unaware of or reject all other tools. To some degree, the most toxic tribalism is that of beginners who don't think of programming languages or techniques as tools and identify themselves with their preferred tools.

We should separate criticism of tools based on legitimate concerns from criticism of tools based on tribal or class issues. Plenty of tools can be used well but largely aren't because most of their devotees are beginners (see: Java, C, C++, Python). Other tools are fundamentally flawed, and while using them well is not impossible, it is a trick that takes a great deal of experience and is beyond the scope of nearly all of its audience (see: PHP, Perl, Javascript). Some tools have lost a great deal of respect because most of their ecosystem is populated by tooling that's orders of magnitude worse than their original design, compounding flaws (see: Java, Javascript, Ruby). Other tools are perfectly fine for what they were designed to do but are almost always used for things they're terrible at (see: Perl, Javascript, Lua, TCL). The popularity of a tool with beginners can certainly negatively affect the suitability of that tool in genuine and valid ways if the beginners are given sufficient control over the tool's later evolution, so it's not as though a tool's popularity with beginners is inherently irrelevant, but a good tool can be used well even as most people use it poorly.

There's another interesting tendency with regard to the popularity of certain tools with beginners, and it's one that's wrapped up with institutions and politics. This is the matter of pedagogy. Java is currently extremely popular, but its popularity owes little to its attributes and much to the fact that it has become part of a standard; there is a curriculum surrounding Java focusing on a Java-centric view of object orientation, and this curriculum forms the basis of both the AP Computer Science curriculum in the United States and various certification and accreditation rules for university programs. In other words, if you live in the United States and you are not an autodidact your first programming experience (barring a bootcamp) will probably be in Java, combined with a curriculum that focuses on UML, inheritance, and the details of Java-style encapsulation, while completely ignoring performance concerns and systematically denying that some problems are not easily represented in an object oriented model. Prior to Java, these programs centered on C++, with a similar set of foci. In other words, for several decades, students with no prior programming experience have been taught that there is one language (Java or C++) and one technique (Java-style OO) that is the best at everything, and as they filter into industry they work with other people who went through the same indoctrination and continue to produce huge ugly monoliths of inefficient Java and C++ "enterprise" code. This is the end-game of letting an echo chamber of like-minded beginners dictate the state of an industry.

So, what do I recommend, with regard to the problem of balkanization in tech pushing out minorities?

I consider this really to be an issue of beginners graduating to higher levels of understanding (and systematic pressure making it harder for certain groups to graduate out of the beginner classification), and one way to help this is to be extremely clear in your criticisms about the nature of the problems you criticize—in other words, rather than saying "PHP users are dumb", say "PHP is a deeply flawed language, and PHP users should be extremely careful when using these particular patterns".

Another way is to make it clear that using a single language is not acceptable in a professional context: any serious developer has a large toolbox already, and if beginners understood that language preference is not a reasonable basis for long-term tribal divisions because any professional belongs to multiple tribes, the toxic identity-based hostility between programming language communities would mostly go away, allowing concrete and issue-based critiques to become more visible.

Also, seasoned developers who frequently work in many languages and have a deep understanding of the positive and negative aspects of many tool designs should become more vocal about tooling: even-handed discussions about this subject make it easier for beginners to graduate into well-rounded developers and avoid making common mistakes that lead to wide-scale disaster.

Finally, standardized programs for computer science education should include language survey courses earlier and feature them more prominently, while removing some of the pro-OO bias that currently characterizes them: nobody should be able to graduate with a CS degree without being truly competent in at least five or six very different languages, rather than the typical gamut of Java, Javascript, and SQL, and they shouldn't graduate without non-trivial exposure to twenty or thirty more. on-communities

Chapter 10

On communities

An extension & refinement of the MOP theory.

See: https://meaningness.com/geeks-mops-sociopaths

The function of any given community is social noise reduction: a community allows groups of people with certain sets of attributes to access each other with fewer "misses"—i.e., without accidentally interacting with a person lacking any of these attributes. (Whether or not this is a good thing depends pretty heavily on the circumstances; however, ultimately, a country club, a Bilderberg conference, a birdwatching forum, and a hackerspace all have in common this basic definition.) Gatekeeping is therefore a huge part of the function of the community.

In a sense, the gatekeeping rules of any community define that community. After all, gatekeeping rules ideally act as a test to ensure that members approximate the ideal community member, but functionally, gatekeeping rules specify who gets into the community and therefore what the range of attributes are of community members. Gatekeeping rules are rarely explicit, and many are inherently implicit: after all, community norms, tolerance for particular community members, and desire to be part of the community all have major gatekeeping ramifications despite never being written or systematically enforced.

Communities are not the result of people coming together so much as they are the result of people seeking a temporary separation by some arbitrary category. They happen naturally, as people congregate toward other people who can fulfill needs and desires. When a community becomes diluted such that different sub-groups within it have different needs, it fractures into multiple communities, whether or not anybody recognizes or points this out for any particular group. Community fracture is always present and fractal to some degree: cliques appear within any community among people who get along better together, and this is part of the community fracture gradient and caused by the same impulse toward sorting. However, all of these organizations are temporary and desire-driven: someone who ceases to be interested in hot rods has left the hot rod community, and communities don't organize along racial lines in the absence of racial tension. The rich and powerful form cliques among themselves because they share attributes that are only accessible to them (nasty gossip about foreign dignitaries isn't available to people who aren't presidents; discussion about how to prevent your kids from murdering you for your inheritance isn't useful for people who have no estate), and pooling power is a side effect rather than a goal.

Prior to complete fracture, a cultural change within a community changes the community's ideals. When somebody leaves a community and calls it "dead"—it's not dead, but it no longer serves the purpose that person needed it for. Communities are tools for solving particular social/interpersonal problems (usually, a desire to communicate about a particular subject), and when community norms change, it's as though someone's screwdriver has been replaced with a hammer.

The MOP theory explains a very specific special case of this phenomenon—one that happens pretty frequently, particularly in "geek" circles. Specifically, it explains what happens when an affinity group organized around a particular subject becomes subverted for the sake of commercial interests. (When we talk about this in terms of Punk, or Star Wars, or comic books, we're really talking about a set of established commercial interests that had already taken over partial control of a social group being subverted by another, larger and more powerful set of commercial interests with different norms.) Whether or not this is a good thing basically comes down to which norms align more closely with the ones you value. While typically the group that takes over has values closer to the notional "mainstream", it's not as though communities haven't been taken over by commercial interests that are even more fringe—as with Palmer-Luckey-funded alt-right trolls infiltrating 4chan. That said, the typical pattern is as mentioned in the MOP theory: a community with a focus on detail and quality has its gatekeeping process subverted by a second group whose focus is on commerce, in such a way that an influx of less-dedicated members become involved; the average dedication level of the group plummets while the most dedicated group members leave the community to form their own. Without the most dedicated members, the infrastructure involved in gatekeeping and in keeping conversations going disappears, leading to most of the casual members also leaving, but enough money has been extracted from the group by commerce-centric outsiders to make this tactic a success.

When a community that has been infiltrated becomes self-sustaining (usually because the new gatekeeping mechanism is sufficiently exclusive that most members still find something valuable in each other's company), it's essentially a new community with new norms: obviously most of the old guard will find this new community less to their liking than the old one, because the old community was based more closely on their own desires and values. It also becomes vulnerable to being infiltrated, split, or subverted by some other commerce-centric group. Whenever a commerce-centric group infiltrates a detail-centric group, the group norms become more lax, because commerce works best at scale and details work best with strong gatekeeping.

While toxic community norms (as mentioned on the Status 451 piece) can become part of gatekeeping, they are rarely truly valuable as such. Communities with toxic norms can become stable so long as they consist primarily of people who can't easily split off. Having been a long-time member of several autism-related internet communities, I can verify that schism doesn't take a huge amount of emotional intelligence or social capital; more typically, toxic norms dominate in groups where confidence in one's ability to split off is low & desire to avoid a toxic community is low—in other words, toxic communities are a result of learned helplesness, not a calculated tactic. it-really-is-better-to-ask-for-permission

Chapter 11

It really is better to ask for permission

A problem with slogans is they get adopted outside of contexts where they make sense, either because the people using them didn't carefully consider whether or not they were true, or because they provide an excuse for doing something that would otherwise not be allowed. Where a monoculture exists, with a group of people with similar values, culture, resources, and problems all make decisions based on the same assumptions, inappropriate slogans can cause systemic biases. The worst offender I'm aware of right now is "it's better to ask for forgiveness than ask for permission".

I have no particular interest in tracking down who said this first and in what context. I will give it the benefit of the doubt and assume that initially it was said in a context where it was true—improv comedy, maybe. However, like similar slogans like "move fast and break things", today it is used almost exclusively in situations where it is not only untrue but also actively harmful.

In order for it to be true for it to be better to ask for forgiveness than permission, the following must also be true:

1. The stakes must be low—in other words, mistakes must not be very damaging (or else apologizing wouldn't be enough)
2. There must be a single homogenous party from which to ask forgiveness (or else asking for forgiveness wouldn't make sense, because you would never be forgiven by all concerned)
3. Asking for permission must be more difficult or risky than getting forgiveness—in other words, the party from which you ask permission must be conservative about it
4. Success must be likely (or else you would be seen as a perpetual screw-up for following this advice)
5. Performing the task must be its own reward—in other words, you must see even the failure as valuable

How this is interpreted, however, hinges on how we define 'better'. When people say this in the tech industry, the most charitable explanation is 'better' means 'better for my paycheck' rather than 'better for users'—in which case, one can expect to apologize to one's supervisor, not one's users, if one takes down all production systems for a week.

While this is charitable, it's hardly an endorsement. None of us should feel better about losing service on the grounds that the developer at fault was forgiven by his supervisor. Any system with users cannot afford the kind of unreliability produced by lack of oversight, because the real stakes are much higher than a single developer's paycheck.

Ultimately, the attitude embedded in this slogan, taken too seriously, is at the core of many of the worst behaviors associated with the tech industry. Uber repeatedly violates labor laws on the grounds that it can get away with doing so—and asks forgiveness when sued. The creepiness of redpillers and PUAs mostly comes down to the entitlement they feel toward other people's bodies, assuming they don't need to worry about consent beforehand because they can ask for forgiveness after they've gotten what they want if in retrospect consent wasn't given. More concretely, this attitude produces shitty dysfunctional code, short-lived companies that sell user data and disappear suddenly, ethically-dubious business practices, and a general culture of "I've got mine, bub" that directly contradicts the phony "save the world" PR everyone likes to wear.

Here's the thing: if you're doing real work, you have real responsibilities. One of your responsibilities is to make sure your decisions are safe—not for your paycheck, but for everyone else. You have the responsibility to check with colleagues in order to make sure your plans aren't stupid and damaging, and you have the responsibility to make sure your colleagues aren't doing anything stupid either. If you aren't willing to take 'no' for an answer, then you should switch to an industry where nothing you do matters, because that's the only situation where such behavior is morally justifiable. context-centric-cultures-call-out-cultures

Chapter 12

Context-centric cultures & call-out cultures

The 'right to be forgotten' addresses a real problem, but does so by making that problem worse. The problem: people are willing to use information taken out of context as a weapon against other people.

This is not a technical problem. It is not a human nature problem. It is a cultural problem: we have allowed misrepresentation (whether deliberate or the result of insufficient effort) to become acceptable.

Misrepresentation should not be a major problem in a world like ours, where more context is more easily accessible than ever before. Technical or UI changes could be made to increase the accessibility of the context, and perhaps that's worth doing, but increased access to context is not going to disincentivize creating and accepting misrepresentations. Misrepresentations are not treated as pieces of useful information to be further integrated, but as weapons. (This is called "call-out culture". It's not a new problem, and it doesn't vary in intensity across the political spectrum.)

The 'right to be forgotten' tries to make out-of-context information useless as a weapon by removing even more context (in a scattershot way, driven by the whims of a corporate approval committee). This addresses one particular aspect of misrepresentation's new increase in popularity—the ability to sift through more data in order to find possible criticisms—but ultimately fails to recognize that the full context is typically easily found & the success of misrepresentation is mostly due to factors that also apply to outright lies. Most misrepresentation is a mixture of out of context truths and complete fabrications—so that someone can point to the out of context truths as a defense of the lies. Too much information is not the problem. The problem is that lack of scrutiny is encouraged when particular types of topics are involved.

An armed society is not necessarily a polite society; however, those armed societies that do not become polite societies descend quickly into violence. Our society is armed more and more with information that, when taken out of context, becomes a weapon; as a result, in the same way communities with guns have cultural norms about trigger discipline, we have a responsibility to maintain cultural norms about context discipline.

To that end, we ought to look at the differences between a context-centric culture (where access to additional context deescalates conflict) and a call-out culture (where access to additional context causes the conflict to escalate).

A context-centric culture has good-faith norms. People who say incorrect things are assumed to be misguided, misinformed, or mistaken, but willing to learn and be corrected. Likewise, people are expected to take criticism in the spirit it is given and consider it carefully. People are expected to always assume that statements are intended as less accusatory or aggressive than they sound. And, people who are unwilling to correct their mistakes or continue to violate boundaries or act too aggressively are excluded from the community or shamed into compliance.

A call-out culture, on the other hand, is characterized by competition for social standing. This competition is waged through accusations, and status is based on the ability to criticize in an entertaining way (regardless of whether or not those criticisms are constructive or even true). People are expected to trust all statements made by the in-group and distrust all statements made by the out-group.

A context-centric culture has a courtesy system based on clearly and accurately indicating the confidence level of statements. Qualifiers are used heavily. Those qualifiers are interpreted as indications of confidence level, and so people who make heavily-qualified statements are not criticized so strongly when those statements are incorrect. However, people are expected to learn from criticism of even heavily-qualified statements: repeating the same heavily-qualified statement after it has been demonstrated to be incorrect is seen as dishonest.

A call-out culture has a courtesy system based on feeding existing power relations. Qualifiers are eschewed. Use of qualifiers is seen as an indication of total lack of confidence, and an absence of confidence is tantamount to weakness. Direct wording is more important than clarity or correctness. Having ever used qualifiers is seen as an indicator of dishonesty, and having ever been incorrect is seen as a sign of weakness and low status. Growth is no excuse.

A context-centric culture takes dangerous ideas very seriously, and carefully refutes them both on their own grounds and in terms of damage to society at large. Dangerous ideas are studied and their strongest points are countered first. Affiliations are discussed, instead of merely hinted at. People who want to damage the community or put it in danger are shamed or excluded entirely, if they cannot be reasoned with.

A call-out culture treats dangerous ideas as part of a calculus of social status, and associates people with them in a haphazard way. How affiliations affect status can change unexpectedly, so they are never made clear. People who want to damage or endanger the community are put in positions of power, if they are sufficiently cut-throat.

A context-centric culture recognizes that other people (including members of the out-group) are in circumstances not fully understood by the speaker. Part of courtesy is getting enough information to determine whether or not saying anything at all is useful. Another part of courtesy is giving people an out—allowing them to exit a discussion without losing status, if they are uncomfortable with it, tired, busy, or simply not in the mood.

A call-out culture considers only the situation of the speaker to be important. All call-outs are moves in a social status game, and their utility is calculated on a personal level—minimax—but never in terms of the good of the society. If the target of a message doesn't respond to accusations louder than the accuser, the accuser wins.

In a context-centric culture, the people with the highest status are kind, careful, quiet, and thoughtful.

In a call-out culture, the people with the highest status are aggressive, reckless, loud, and stupid.

A context-centric culture has multiple spaces, each with its own rules. Visitors are expected to obey the rules of these spaces and to be mindful of the boundaries between them.

A call-out culture has multiple spaces, each with their own rules, but it is treated as though it were flat. Visitors are expected to criticize residents for not following the rules of the visitors' own favorite spaces, and to treat the residents of other spaces as easy targets for accusations.

In a context-centric culture, discussion deescalates conflict because people try to understand each other.

In a call-out culture, discussion is conflict because people try to defeat each other.

How do we get from a call-out culture to a context-centric culture? It requires a collective willingness to no longer put up with misrepresentation & drama hounds, and a collective discipline about fact-checking and good-faith assumptions. We will need to begin expecting people to read the entire article before posting a comment, and to read the entire existing comment thread before adding their own. We will need to begin criticizing people for low-effort comments in a way that encourages them to intellectually engage, and we will need to make a practice of deescalation. We will need to stop boosting sick burns and start boosting great discussion. And, we will need to start acting with the recognition that we don't know the whole story. a-libertarian-case-for-social-justice

Chapter 13

A libertarian case for social justice

A consistent & desirable libertarian ethical philosophy is possible, and indeed, it exists: existential ethics, as articulated by Jean-Paul Sartre and Simone de Bouvoir, centers upon self-knowledge, personal responsibility (in the form of good-faith acceptance of one's freedom & the responsibility that comes with it), and the maximization of the personal freedom of both oneself and others. What Sartre & Bouvoir's work has that's lacking in shallower but more popular attempts at libertarian ethical philosophy like Rand's is a nuanced understanding of the impact of actually-existing power structures.

Acting as though our world is already equitable prevents the world from becoming equitable, in the same way that a poor person who acts as though he is already rich will only dig himself further into debt. A serious libertarian (as opposed to a libertarian of convenience) is invested in a more equitable world, where the freedoms he experiences are available to others, and where opportunity for advancement is there for those who take it. As a result, such a person must be very careful to avoid prefigurative politics.

It's possible to be sheltered from the knowledge of existing inequities. Consider the notion of a 'gentleman' in enlightenment europe: regardless of actual income, all 'gentlemen' were considered basically alike in dignity & were subject to social rules built on that percieved equality (including forgiveness for certain kinds of mischef). Gentlemen helped each other out. The function of duelling was related to this status: a gentleman would only duel another gentleman, but the primary kind of insult that would trigger a duel was the suggestion that someone ought not to be considered a member of this class—in other words, demands to duel were an assertion that one belongs to the club, and accepting such a demand constituted an apology in itself for an attempt at exile. The social rules that these folks lived by ignored and ameliorated actual inequality between them in terms of access to resources, and in many cases acted to prevent members who were down on their luck from needing to perform unaristocratic tasks like working for a living.

A libertarianism of gentlemen is easy: such a group, their resources provided by a massive underclass and their equality and freedom provided by a social contract that provides access to these resources based on need, can negotiate as though they were really equals. But, ultimately, that equality is based on charity (socially enforced). Gentlemen are provided the privilege to believe that their fragile equality is strong and their status is earned, because social norms within their community insulate them from the source of their freedom. (As Robert Anton Wilson notes, 'privilege' is latin for 'private law', and every community has its own norms for its own members.)

A libertarianism of gentlemen can easily, without any kind of malice, slide into oligarchy. Indeed, this appears to occur whenever awareness of actually-existing power imbalances is ignored. When someone with power acts as though their freedom is shared by someone who lacks it, it becomes a situation of 'personal responsibility for thee, but not for me': contracts that would be acceptable between true equals have hidden violence, because free choices are made based on an understanding of consequences, and one party is stuck in a permanent double-bind where (unless they are very lucky, very careful, and very persistent) even the best choice is a bad one and all choices lead to fewer choices down the road.

This compounds: power acts as a lever to amplify the benefits of all choices, and a cushion to limit the impact of all failures, but the source of that power is the limited choices of other people, who are the source of the amplified benefits and bear the brunt of the impact of failures. Power makes it easier to accumulate more power, and it is taken by folks who have less, often in ways that are hidden or easily ignored. This is desirable to a libertarian-of-convenience (who wishes for their own personal possibility space to be maximized, even at the cost of that of others, and even when they have no justification for their privilege beyond accidents of birth), but to a serious libertarian (who desires to maximize both total choice & the choices available to the average person—to maximize human potential, human flourishing, and human freedom), this is a crime.

There's a slogan associated with libertarianism: "my freedom to swing my fist ends where your nose begins". This is to say: libertarians want to maximize personal freedom to the extent that their choices do not do violence to other people. A serious and intellectually honest libertarian will recognize that power is an amplifier for violence: what constitutes a harmless prank between gentlemen could ruin the life of a servant, so a serious libertarian will take into account the situation of those around him when determining what does and does not constitute violence.

This is a difficult task. It's much easier to assume everybody is in the same boat as you are, and one might be tempted to act this way out of laziness. But, for a serious libertarian, avoiding violence against one's peers is imperative (even when that violence is accidental), and allowing others to become one's equal is just as important as maximizing one's own ability to make decisions.

This is where social justice comes in. Despite widespread misrepresentations & occasional misuse, ideas about social justice are a set of tools for attempting to understand actually-existing power structures and ameliorate their effects so that people from different walks of life can interact on an equal footing.

Some are tools for understanding power structures: intersectionality helps us understand how different experiences interact, so that we can understand power imbalances in a more fine-grained way than simply identifying people with a single group & treating that group monolithically. Others are tools for leveling the playing field for communication: a safe space is a temporary set of rules for making honest communication possible when power imbalances would otherwise encourage people to self-censor (and safe spaces are tailored to the circumstances they are intended for: a safe space for sexual expression cannot be the same as a safe space for supporting survivors of sexual trauma, for instance, since the former explicitly allows the free expression of rape fantasies & other material that the latter must enforce social norms against). Still others are tools for allowing people with particular emotional needs to participate in conversations: trigger warnings allow people with PTSD to prepare themselves for a conversation about a sensitive subject that, were they unprepared, they might have an extreme and discussion-derailing reaction to.

All tools in the social justice toolbox are experiments, constantly being tinkered with by people who are trying to figure out the best way to maximize personal freedom in situations where doing so isn't easy.

One does not need to agree that all these tools are effective or useful. However, a serious libertarian will consider the concerns these tools are meant to address & at least apply tools to try to address those same concerns—and any tools intended to address those concerns will be, by definition, tools of social justice. To avoid social justice is to out oneself as libertarian-in-name-only, unconcerned with the personal liberty of others. the-language-around-free-speech-in-civil-libertarian-circles-is-flawed

Chapter 14

The language around free speech in civil-libertarian circles is flawed

There's something that bothers me about the way we talk about speech. By 'we', I mean not just self-defined anarchists but the broader scope of civil-libertarians, from the EFF to the ACLU.

There are terms like "chilling effects" that, in denotation, are really well-defined, but in connotation are almost dog whistles. We cause a chilling effect when we create an environment where saying certain things has a social cost, and this is basically always framed as bad. But, it's also a useful tool—when we create a code of conduct, set ground rules for our own spaces, encourage etiquette, or give someone a dirty look when they behave boorishly, we are using chilling effects to discourage certain kinds of mostly-communicative behaviors.

If you're using soft power to shape the way people communicate in order to make a society work better, that's an improvement over using hard power to police speech, from the perspective of anybody who might violate it in good faith, right? Having soft-power-oriented structures in place lets people choose to violate them when they feel like they must, & lets them change if it's decided they're counterproductive. It ultimately has the flexibility that hard power lacks: the upper limit on punishment is solitude, and each person chooses the extent to which they agree with enforcement.

So, the bigger deal is identifying soft power and understanding it *as* power. And, we do that pretty well in many cases (though newbie anarchists often don't).

The freeze peach crowd does it well too, but can't distinguish soft power used toward positive ends from soft power used toward negative ends (or sometimes can't distinguish soft power from hard power). It makes sense: after all, when it's used in the context of an existing hierarchical dynamic based on hard power, and acts in conjunction with the threat of heavily imbalanced hard power, it acts as a threat toward those who go against the system. Nobody wants to get a chilling effect produced by the FBI or FSB, because ignoring it might mean a death sentence, and organizations who are used to looking at environments where a few powerful actors dominate media (such as, well, every environment prior to around 2005) will get strange results if they apply their normal tools of analysis to equitable groups with power ratios hovering around 1.

If a group decides, collectively, to write a code of conduct that discourages certain kinds of speech, this is fundamentally different from a government writing a law that forbids certain kinds of speech. For one, the consequences are not comparable: the most the group can do is refuse to let you in (and for every constraint in some group's code of conduct, you can find another group without that constraint or with that constraint reversed), while a government can imprison you or kill you. For another, forgiveness is collective in the case of the group: if as little as a third of the members of an equitable group decide that what you did was OK, the letter of the law ceases to matter, because you can avoid coming into contact with the rest; in the case of a government, forgiveness has a single point of failure & a structure designed to punish anyone who acts upon forgiveness at lower levels. For instance, Edward Snowden could not return to the United States even if nearly everyone decided he was in the right, unless he got a pardon from the president; if he tried, anybody who helped him would be liable to be imprisoned.

Getting rid of the state (or even tuning its presence in our lives down to a dull roar) means needing to understand how to wield soft power to cultivate the health of your community, and knowing if and when hard power becomes necessary. A big part of that is going to be getting rid of the idea that soft power is inherently cowardly or dishonest.

I don't think soft power is even particularly subtle—and I'm autistic, for fuck's sake. It becomes obvious if you look for it.

When it comes down to it, soft power means human flexibility over rules-lawyering, and that means that bans are replaced with chilling effects. That's what progress toward humane consensus-based self-governance looks like. on-tackiness

Chapter 15

On tackiness

Tackiness is a moral issue, in the sense that it identifies free-riders. This is why it's punished so harshly.

Tackiness is a quality we attribute to any action that produces cultural capital without actually benefitting the community as a whole. We're wired to punish tackiness the same way we punish other kinds of 'cheating'.

(The special case of social class in tackiness is something I won't get into too much. Suffice to say that conspicuous consumption has weaponized anti-tackiness reflexes in order to destroy social mobility.)

Social groups (and media) are characterized, to outsiders, by their tackiest elements. The reason is that people who optimize for social capital to the exclusion of all else tend to get it (if only temporarily). Whoever in your group has the greatest self-promotion to group-benefit ratio (whoever is tackiest) will end up being the public face of your group, because everybody else is content to communicate among themselves and follow social rules. Only the tacky actually break through the edges of the group while embodying (a distorion of) group norms, as a side effect of trying to saturate the consciousness of the whole group.

Case in point: I joined Twitter in 2006. Hashtag use was never 'normal' among regular users. Using it felt tacky if not slimy. However, since hashtags are an amplifier, people who did use them became loudest. They came to characterize the platform to outsiders. As the platform grew, outsiders became new users, and they acted the way that they had been told twitter users acted (which is to say, they thought normal users were expected to act like marketroids and spambots). Thus, the new users got louder, and shouted over reasonable regular conversation.

How do you prevent that? One way is to ensure that tacky behavior is not merely socially punished but actually technically only marginally effective.

I think the fediverse (the federated social network formed by Gnu Social, Mastodon, and others using the ActivityPub and OpenSocial standards) does this relatively effectively: behavior is isolated to particular groups, and it takes more effort to hop between groups. Because of this, the ability for a message to get 'outside' depends fairly heavily on catering to the needs of the regular users, who feel a sense of ownership and protectiveness around their communities. Attention-seeking messages don't have the same kind of edge on community-serving messages in terms of expected attention that they would on Twitter. Furthermore, because metrics are typically hidden, it's slightly harder to carefully tune messages for virality. on-revolutionary-ideas

Chapter 16

On revolutionary ideas

Revolutionary ideas always are masked as a return to older ideas or appeal to common sense only because they can't be expressed without the intellectual groundwork that makes them seem inevitable once fully comprehended.

This is because teaching (as opposed to more concrete forms of communication) is a kind of augmented independent discovery. If someone can be told something & understand it, it was trivial. For serious ideas, the learner redisovers them.

The role of the teacher is to create an artificial mental/rhetorical environment where the rediscovery of the principle is much more likely, and repeatedly lead the horse to water—because non-trivial ideas cannot be unambiguously expressed.

This means that, in a very real way, to become popular, revolutionary ideas can no longer be revolutionary: the prerequisites for finding them obvious must be floating around in the environment.

Someone with a mental one wit landscape that diverges sufficiently from the monoculture will have unique insights simply because they are building on combinations of ideas unavailable to their peers.

We call these people geniuses, but their genius can be engineered through cosmopolitanism.

The common pattern that they aren't appreciated in their own time is not because of some scientific telos but because geniuses are by definition out of step with their environment, and we can often find figures that are in step with ours.

(In other words, not only are geniuses not appreciated in their own time, but it's exceedingly unlikely for them ever to be appreciated, unless the future mainstream happens to coincide with their own mental landscape enough for them to be understood)

One way to counteract this: if you have an idea, make it possible to explain the foundations of the idea in as accessible a way as possible.

You still run into the Periodic Table problem where cultural bigotry discourages people who could understand from bothering—because your references and foundations are part of the outgroup's signals and thus it mustn't be admitted that they have value. Imagination & the distribution of development

A popular idea is that 'Japan is from the future'—that technology there as a whole is more advanced. This is probably the inspiration for the much-overused Gibson quote "the future is here, but it is not fully distributed". In reality, Japan has what TVTropes would call 'schizo tech': affordable personal robots are available and toilets have bidets and mp3 players, but offices still use fax machines instead of email and documents get distributed on paper by couriers.

Schizo tech is truth in television: every culture's advancement levels look inconsistent and lopsided from the outside, because what you invest in is based on what you value & what is made easy to improve. More specific & accurate than 'the future isn't evenly distributed' is 'development in a field is proportional to the means of development'—most importantly, the means of imagination (the prerequisites for accurately imagining potential practical solutions to problems).

The means of imagination include:

• attention (you have to think about problems to solve them, usually),

• incentives (need, profitability),

• and path dependence (do the resources you already have make solving the problem easy, and does the way you talk & think about the resources make it easy to imagine that solution).

Sometimes these things come together: Japanese robotics tech was driven by a government program to fund research in robotics caused by a projected need to care for the aging population in their old age, and was paired with a new emphasis on STEM education in the 70s and 80s. Sometimes they don't: startups that make sense in the bay area often don't scale beyond it because the needs of very rich but time-starved developers are really strange.

One of the reason that 'scenius' (i.e., the particular creative culture of social groups) matters so much is that norms, values, and availability biases strongly affect the sense of the adjacent possible.

The intellectual trajectory of the 20th century largely came out of a handful of people who moved from Germany & Austria to New Jersey ("the Martians" of the Institute for Advanced Study—Godel, Von Neumann, Einstein) and their friends, who set into motion a new reevaluation of all the old 19th century certainties about the universe (the consistency of time and space across reference points, the solidity of the matter-energy distinction, the role of probability as a mere useful tool rather than an essential property of physical law, the completeness and consistency of mathematics)[1]. The technical trajectory of the 20th century largely came out of a couple communities of researchers in conversation with this tradition—the theoretical basis of computing developed by Church and Turing on the basis of Godel's work and feeding it back to Von Neumann's circle in their work on building computers to simulate hydrogen bombs [2], Bell Labs (through their internal Bell Technical Journal) combining IAS's work on quantum mechanics with their own work on materials science to produce transistors and communications satellites[3], Xerox PARC in conversation both with Bell Labs and with revolutionary ideas about education and politics coming out of information theory & cybernetics by way of places like Dartmouth and University of Illinois[4]... There is a material basis for this as well, in the form of a consistent effort by the US government to pay very smart people to hang out in places like IAS or work on projects like PLATO and the ARPAnet, combined with increased funding for STEM in the immediate wake of Sputnik[5]. In other words, access to a variety of revolutionary ideas was combined with social connections and insulation from the need to make quick & shallow progress, and as a result, deep progress occurred.

This ability to imagine new practical solutions controls the shape of society. Our communications with each other today are biased by the communications media developed during this golden age from about 1910 to 1975 of radical uncertainty and radical intellectual community, and the priorities of these folks (often unexamined, and not always the same as our own) influence the kinds of thoughts we are capable of thinking, the kinds of possibilities we are capable of imagining, and therefore the kinds of futures we are capable of bringing about.

Expanding the means of imagination has historically been done at state or institutional scale: finding smart people from across the world, bringing them together, filling the lower floors of their pyramid of needs using large quantities of cash. The inability of Google & Apple to produce and maintain a PARC-like productivity demonstrates that time, absence of pressure, and influx of truly radical ideas are vital components of this alchemical marriage—merely putting smart people together in a building & keeping them fed will not create miracles, so long as they are expected to ship.

There's one way to seize the means of imagination that doesn't take big (i.e., centralized) resource allocation: access to information outside the usual bubble. New or previously-unknown theories & models (even if wrong), alternative models (even if prototype or design fiction), unexpected messages (even if random—ex., by cartomancy), and altered states or unusual constraints can stimulate the imagination by breaking the sense of the adjacent possible out of a strict path dependence with the kind of financial, time, and effort investment accessible to many individuals.

[1] See: Stranger Than We Can Imagine by John Higgs
[2] See: Turing's Cathedral by George Dyson
[3] See: The Idea Factory by Jon Gertner
[4] See: Tools for Thought by Howard Rheingold and A People's History of Computing in the United States by Joy Lisi Rankin
[5] See: The Friendly Orange Glow by Brian Dear
Note: this essay was originally called Imagination and the Distribution of Futurity until I realized that 'futurity' meant something else. on-infohazards

Chapter 17

On infohazards

\marginpar{This post is adapted from a conversation on secure scuttlebutt at %+3IwyiasfP+l+TRBvxIeUV56wlnZHNzCx6veYfPvk2o=.sha256}

An infohazard is a discrete piece of information that, by itself, causes major, fundamental shifts in your worldview. It does not need to be true, or meaningful. Bostrom provides a more detailed taxonomy.

It's a common theme in fiction—particularly horror fiction & the 'weird'. For instance, the "Yellow Sign" in the play-within-the-book The King in Yellow causes those who see it to become thralls to the titular King, and the play of the same name in that book causes anyone who reads its fragments to go mad. Likewise, the infohazard is a common element in Lovecraft's work, usually as media, although in Facts Concerning the Late Arthur Jerimyn & His Family, it is a secret about the protagonist's ancestry. However, the infohazard is not unique to horror fiction—it also appears in theology (for instance, in the form of the magical properties of the true name of god & the ability for a mental image of the ain sof to physically blind people, in jewish theology).

Infohazards are necessarily rare: humans have extremely well-developed defenses against even small changes to how they think about the world. World-changing ideas—things that could have qualified as infohazards had understanding them truly implied accepting their implications (like natural selection, for instance)—typically do not manage to fully circulate, even among professionals, until a generation dies off and a new batch (for whom the world-shaking revelation is common sense) takes its place.

Nevertheless, we have a couple real-life candidates for things that were once potent infohazards:

• Cantor's continuity conjecture—which both Godel & Cantor spent months trying to prove or disprove before succumbing to death related to ongoing mental illness

• Godel's incompleteness theorem—which was probably at least partially implicated in the stress-induced paranoid flare-up that caused his death (although he was working on the continuity conjecture at the time)

• Some core ideas of the french existentialists (for instance: the idea that the world is without inherent meaning & any telos is our own invention)

• Roko's basilisk (which, when unleashed on a community who had been spending years reasoning about the mechanisms that make it operate, caused a panic)

• Plato's theory of forms (which inverts & externalizes the mental model as a directly-perceived eternal domain upon which the real world is said to have been modeled) and Cartesian dualism (which reifies the mind as immaterial) —both of which, like herpes simplex, have infected basically the whole human population

On the more concrete side, there are some images that due to their structure cause permanent or semi-permanent visual damage.

Candidates for still-live infohazards include the collected essays of Nick Land.

The fortean (or high strangeness) is distinct from the infohazard in a few ways. One is that where an infohazard disrupts existing categories and assumptions and produces new ones, high strangeness is merely resistant to categorization.

Things can be both, for sure! A lot of close encounters are both fortean (in the sense that they don't hang together in a way that is amenable to rational thought) and info-hazardous (in the sense that the people who experience them end up undergoing rapid personality change). Usually, this is the result of an attempt to figure out under what ontology would these experiences make sense. (For an extreme example, see Philip K. Dick's Exegesis, or the collected writing of Witley Streiber, or read Rigorous Intuition.)

Sometimes there's not enough information to even make guesses: for instance, the Simonson case (described by Jacques Vallee & later by Robert Anton Wilson), wherein a craft landed in a man's back yard, the crew of the craft asked him for a pitcher of water, and they proceeded to make him some whole-wheat pancakes with the water and then leave. (This is my favorite example of high strangeness because it's also not particularly numinous the way that most instances of it are. It's merely essentially inexplicable: any possible explanation of the crew of saucer-shaped flying craft making random folks free pancakes but forgetting to bring their own water is in contradiction with way too many things we all believe about reality.) spanning-problem-space

Chapter 18

Spanning problem-space

Determining how best to improve one's own suite of mental models & thinking tools is a hard problem: we can't easily see ideas beyond the horizon, and ideas we haven't yet invested effort in developing are distorted at best, but determining the value of ideas is necessary because of the scarcity of time & other resources. This is further complicated by the fact that knowledge-seeking is not a single-player game: everyone is constantly refining their suite of mental models, making decisions based on them, and producing material that makes certain ideas more or less accessible, and the value of a mental model is determined in part by the people who share it or share adjacent models, in somewhat complicated ways.

My current idea of how best to improve the value of one's suite of mental models is based on a couple assumptions:

1. Ideas are adjacent to each other in semantic space based on shared attributes.
2. It is easier to learn an idea if it is adjacent to an idea you've already learned. The ease with which an idea is learned is proportional to the number of adjacent ideas already learned.
3. Adjacency in semantic space, seen as a network, is a web, not a tree. Some ideas are adjacent to each other even when none of their immediate peers are adjacent—such as when seemingly unrelated ideas in seemingly distinct fields have striking similarities.
4. A factor in the value of an idea is its adjacency to other valuable ideas. Part of this is ease of communication: when we have a shared terminology and set of assumptions with people, we can share new ideas more easily. When we share few ideas with someone, communicating with them is difficult.
5. Another factor in the value of an idea is its concrete utility, in of itself. For instance, the set of ideas known as ballistics are very useful in predicting the movement of objects.
6. A third factor in the value of an idea is its scarcity. Someone who is an expert in an obscure field will have greater social capital than someone

who is an expert in a more commonly-understood field with the same concrete utility adjacent to ideas of comparable value.

7. Some ideas have as their primary concrete utility the capacity to change the value of other ideas by changing something about society. Rhetoric, for instance, can be used to modify ideas about the value of certain other ideas, thus changing things like salary and social capital.

8. Adjacent ideas are not always obvious. Sometimes they are only obvious in retrospect.

9. Adjacency doesn't necessarily have any relationship to truth or intent, although systematic biases (including toward truth or toward consistency) may favor clusters of similar ideas. For instance, mathematics, because it enforces consistency, finds large numbers of similar patterns in far-flung contexts.

10. Traditional (tree-like) academic paths through idea space are easy to traverse in part because so much effort has gone into lowering traversal effort—the production of teaching material, specialized terminology, and communities and social structures (such as universities). That same ease of traversal lowers the value because it increases the number of people with nearly identical mental toolkits.

11. Autodidacts trade the easy-to-traverse yet diluted conventional path for unconventional connections of unknown value. They risk missing ideas that are relatively hard to pick up without structural aid but that are very useful for opening up further vistas or closing off dead ends (like calculus, or godel's incompleteness).

12. Successful autodidacts are polymaths. Unsuccessful autodidacts are cranks. It's hard to tell the difference without mastery of related fields.

13. Undiscovered or undocumented adjacencies between seemingly unrelated subjects are common, but few have much concrete utility. However, those that do are extremely valuable.

14. As a result, someone can optimize the value of their mental toolkit by following traditional paths enough to enable communication but otherwise specifically choosing to persue seemingly unrelated subjects that are rarely persued together, periodically attempting to synthesize them. Random number generators are useful in path choice and synthesis, since the likelihood of producing an unconventional path and the likelihood of choosing paths with hidden adjacencies are both high.

silicon-valley-hasnt-innovated-since-1978

Chapter 19

Silicon Valley hasn't innovated since 1978

I'm serious. Name one thing in computing that showed up after 1978 that wasn't either an incremental improvement on a pre-1978 technology or a crappier but cheaper version of a pre-1978 technology. I'm not trying to produce sophistry here. There's a huge difference in the level of novelty of original research in computing tech during the span 1940–1980 and the level of novelty in the same after 1980, & it relates directly to economics.

From 1940 to 1980, computer science was being done by folks with doctorates & experience in other disciplines, funded by government money to do pure research & moonshot shit—especially ARPA funding starting in the wake of Sputnik for ed-tech. When that funding dried up, so did productivity in original research, because the ability to continue to be employed depended on profitability in a consumer market (which means racing to market... which means avoiding risky detours).

The exact same people have drastically different productivity levels with the two models. Kay at PARC in the 70s went from having seen a sketchpad demo to having a complete functioning live-editable GUI with network transparency in 10 years, because of government ed-tech money. In the early 80s, Kay moved to Atari & tried to continue the kind of work he had been doing. And then he got laid off, and went to Apple, got laid off again. The work he started in the 70s has been treading water because short term profits can't support deep research.

This isn't to say that what has happened since isn't valuable. The computing technologies developed prior to 1980 have mostly become cheap enough that they have become accessible to a mass audience, in part because of iteration on manufacturing techniques, & mostly because of cheap labor (in the form of fresh-out-of-college CS students who will write bad code for half of what you'd pay the PhDs to refuse to write bad code, and will work unpaid overtime if you give them a ball pit and a superiority complex). But, using 70s tech to make 60s tech bigger (ex., deep neural networks) isn't innovation—it's doing the absolute most obvious thing under the circumstances, which is all that can be defended in a context of short-term profitability.

What armies of clerks were doing in the 30s was 'computation', sure, but it's very different. The pointing devices we use, the look and feel of our UIs, and our UI metaphors haven't changed since the 70s except in terms of resolution. Our network protocols haven't much either.

This is to say:

Somebody who had used an Alto in 1979 could travel through time and sit down at a modern PC and know basically how to do most tasks—they would think of a modern PC as a faster but less featureful stripped down Alto clone, like the Star was. They could probably even code on it—they would have been familiar with UNIX shells & C, & with SGML-style markup. They would find it disappointingly awkard compared to Interlisp-D and Smalltalk environments they're used to, but they could make it work.

Meanwhile, to somebody from 1940, home computer tech of 1980 would be mind-blowing. Such a person, even if they were in computing, would not be familiar with the concept of a programming language (since stored program computers didn't exist yet).

The VC model ties into this difference. The best possible outcome, under the VC model, is that actual costs are low & the VCs get wild profits in the short term, after which they sell their stakes & don't need to care anymore. The easiest & most reliable way to do that is a ponzi scheme (or, to be more technically correct, the pyramid-selling of hype—in this case, to other, marginally less savvy investors). With enough cash floating around, you can keep a company that provides no service & has no income afloat indefinitely, and everyone involved becomes a paper millionaire.

The goal of ARPA from '57 to '78 was quite different: to encourage children to become engineers in order to have an edge in a high-tech hot-war that never really ended up coming, and to build tech that lets them bootstrap new tech more easily. Massive short-term losses in that. (It obviously didn't exactly work: we did end up getting a lot of cheap engineers, but few of them had the background to be able to more-than-iteratively improve upon the tech they grew up on, even had they been allowed to by management.)

The difference in development between the first 40 years of CS and the second 40 is absolutely not the result of the low-hanging fruit all being picked. The most interesting technical work is being done by individuals and small groups still. Important features & useful tools that were well known in the late 70s are actually missing from modern tech because of gaps in education & because having them prevents some avenues toward monetization. (Ex., you can't live-edit software if the software is closed source.)

I really hate the "silicon valley is a center of innovation" memeplex & feel the need to inject some historical context whenever I see it. It's weird, masturbatory, Wired Magazine bullshit & it leads to the lionization of no-talent con artists like Steve Jobs. Making money & making tech are very different skills, often fundamentally at odds: good tech is very often not profitable and the most profitable tech is just varying reframings of rentseeking. Very few people can do both well, and SV has a bias toward profit. Because of this, in most cases, the product isn't actually the tech but the techwashing. Apple's an excellent case in point. After they dropped the Apple] [line, their main product was hype & terminology stolen from PARC with a free underpowered home computer thrown in (for the low low price of 8 grand).

In an environment where cash is king, when you can make bank on PR, it's foolish to try to innovate—and the valley has learned this lesson better than it has learned anything else.